Life Inside the Arctic Circle

by Sam Brelsfoard

PEARSON

Scott
Foresman

Editorial Offices: Glenview, Illinois • Parsippany, New Jersey • New York, New York
Sales Offices: Needham, Massachusetts • Duluth, Georgia • Glenview, Illinois
Coppell, Texas • Ontario, California • Mesa, Arizona

ISBN: 0-328-13638-7

4 5 6 7 8 9 10 V0G1 14 13 12 11 10 09 08 07 06

Geography of the Arctic Circle

The Arctic Circle is defined by an imaginary boundary line that encircles Earth's northernmost region. Some scientists estimate the location of the Arctic Circle by looking for the tree line.

As the climate becomes colder the farther north you go, the forests thin out. The trees become shorter. Eventually, there is a point where trees no longer grow. This is called the tree line. In areas north of the tree line, trees cannot get what they need to grow.

The North Pole's polar ice cap, Greenland, and parts of Canada make up the majority of the Arctic. Parts of Norway, Finland, Sweden, Iceland, the United States, and Russia are inside the Arctic Circle as well. People can only live in a small part of this area due to the extreme weather. However, there are still areas inside the Arctic Circle that some people call home.

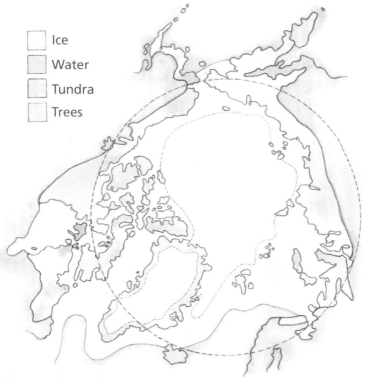

Ice
Water
Tundra
Trees

This map shows the northernmost part of Earth, where the Arctic Circle is.

Habitable areas inside the Arctic Circle can be found in all of the countries within its borders. The Aleuts live in western Alaska. Inuit people, such as the Iñupiaq, live in northern Alaska. The Yup'ik live in the southwestern part of Alaska south of the Arctic Circle. Other Inuit people live in northern Canada and Greenland.

The word *Inuit* describes many different groups of people who live north of the Arctic line. In addition to Canada, they can be found in many other countries within the Arctic Circle.

Their cultures have been present in the Arctic Circle for thousands of years. In the past, they have depended on the hunting of animals such as caribou, seals, and whales to feed their families and even build their homes. As modern technology makes its way north of the Arctic line, they are finding new ways to live.

Polar bear

Caribou

The red on this map shows where some Inuit and other arctic people claim territorial rights in Alaska, Canada, Russia, and Greenland.

Many animals make their home in the Arctic as well. The caribou, the musk ox, the arctic fox, and the arctic hare all live on the cold landscape. A variety of animals, such as seals, walruses, whales, polar bears, and arctic char spend their time in the water. Char are fish related to trout and salmon.

Winter is harsh in the Arctic. The animals that live there are adapted to the cold in many different ways. Some, like the arctic hare and fox, have thick fur. Others, like walruses and whales, have a layer of blubber, or fat. Still, others, like caribou, move below the tree line or hibernate when the arctic winter blows in.

Arctic seal

The Environment

The weather in the Arctic Circle is usually very cold and snowy. Winters in the Arctic are very long, and summers are short and cool. Permafrost covers all of the ground that is not ice. Permafrost is hard, frozen land. Only a small amount of soil above the permafrost thaws in the summer months. Much of the ground stays frozen all year long.

The cold is not the only thing that makes the Arctic different from other areas of the world. Because of the angle of Earth's axis, in certain areas during the summer there is a long period when the sun does not set.

At the Arctic Circle, the sun will not set for an entire day. This happens on June 21. The farther north you travel, the longer the sun stays in the sky.

The North Pole has the longest period of time without a sunset. It is the northernmost part of the Arctic Circle. For six months in the summer there is constant daylight. In the winter it is completely dark for another six months!

Because the sun stays in the sky for six months, the Arctic has been nicknamed the "Land of the Midnight Sun." In some areas of Alaska an alarm sounds at ten o'clock at night to let the local children know it is time to go home. Without this signal, it would be difficult for some people to know the time. It always looks like it's the middle of the day. This is a good example of how cultures of the Arctic have adapted to their environment.

The Arctic Circle includes the North Pole.

The Athabaska Glacier in Alberta, Canada

The Arctic Tundra

Tundra is the area that forms a belt around the Arctic Ocean. The tundra begins north of the tree line, where trees no longer grow. Here you find permafrost.

The permafrost lies just under the surface of the earth. It covers the land and makes it impossible for trees to grow there. As mentioned previously, permafrost is a layer of permanently frozen soil. In fact, vegetation only grows on most areas of the tundra for six to ten weeks during the summer. Due to low temperatures and high winds, snowfall in the winter is actually helpful. It helps to **insulate** plants from severe cold. Animals that hibernate, or sleep, during the winter use the snow pack to keep warm as well.

The diorama of the Arctic Circle illustrates how the land might look in the Arctic.

The animals that live within the Arctic Circle year-round and do not hibernate have their own ways of surviving in the cold climate. The arctic fox has thick insulating fur to help it keep warm. Birds like the willow ptarmigan have thick, downy feathers to protect them.

The arctic hare also has a thick coat of fur. It has smaller ears than other types of hares so that less of its skin is exposed. The arctic hare is an herbivore and eats grass and plants during the warmer summer months. When snow covers the ground in the winter, heather becomes its primary food source.

Some animals do not stay in the Arctic Circle all year. Caribou, which are also called reindeer, move south of the tree line when the weather turns cold. This way, they can find food that becomes scarce in the Arctic.

The arctic fox has thick insulating fur to keep it warm in the frigid temperatures.

History of the Arctic People

Human cultures have adapted to life in the Arctic as well. Settlements can be found on all of the continents that touch the Arctic Circle, including North America.

More than fifteen thousand years ago, people from Asia migrated across the Bering Land Bridge, which stretched between Russia and Alaska and connected Asia to North America. They settled in what is now known as Alaska and Canada. Some eventually moved farther south, but some stayed within the Arctic Circle.

When the Inuit first arrived, they had to learn to adjust to the harsh life on the tundra very quickly. The Norse people experienced the same challenges when they first settled in Iceland after A.D. 860. Both groups of settlers learned to survive in their own ways. For instance, to protect themselves from the severe arctic conditions, they made clothes out of the skins of native animals.

Today, about four million people live within the Arctic Circle. Some groups of people have been there for many generations. Their ancestors may go all the way back to the time when the Bering Land Bridge still existed. Others have moved there from southern areas more recently.

Historically, the Arctic peoples were hunters, gatherers, fishermen, and herders. Some followed caribou, while others learned how to make canoes for fishing. For some of those who can trace their family trees back to the first settlers, these roles have not changed at all.

For others, however, daily life has changed to keep up with modern lifestyles and technology. The ways of the modern world have mixed with their traditions.

An Inuit village north of the Arctic Circle

Inuit Peoples

The Iñupiaq of Alaska, and the Yup'ik from Siberia are examples of Inuit peoples. The word *Eskimo* was once used to describe these groups. Now *Inuit* is considered more appropriate. The word *Inuit* simply means "people." The word *Eskimo* means "eaters of raw meat." This Algonquin word was an insult, and it is no longer used for the people who live in the Arctic.

Inuit groups live in what most people consider to be **isolation.** Their surroundings might be thought of as brutal. They have adapted their lifestyles to their environments by learning how to live off of the land and the sea.

The Inuit have also undergone many changes in their way of life in order to keep up with the modern world. In the following pages we will see how different Inuit peoples, as well as other cultures, have changed their lives to fit the Arctic.

Inuit children

Aleut

The Aleut people live in the Aleutian Islands, a chain of islands that extend for about one thousand miles off the western coast of Alaska. The Aleut have a lot in common with the Inuit of Alaska, though they have a separate culture. They have learned to take advantage of the sea, their biggest resource. They learned to build boats and are expert fishermen.

Before the 1700s Aleuts lived in small, scattered villages throughout western Alaska and the Aleutian Islands. They survived the harsh weather by building houses that were partially underground.

Aleuts have adjusted to the modern economy, yet they keep many of their own traditions. Fishing is still a very important part of their culture. It is both a business for the Aleuts and a way to get their own food.

The Aleuts are skilled boat builders.

Chukchi

The Chukchi people live on the Asian side of the North Pacific. They are the largest group of indigenous people in the area. Their name comes from a Russian word meaning "rich in reindeer."

They are divided into two primary groups. One group traditionally herds reindeer for their milk, hides, and meat. They live away from the sea in northern Russia. This group depends on these animals for survival.

The other group lives on the Arctic and Bering seacoasts. They survive by hunting marine mammals, such as seals, walruses, and fish.

The two groups have adapted their lives in similar areas in very different ways. However, both groups use the area's natural resources as much as they can.

Some Chukchi people herd reindeer.

Athabasca

Around 8000 B.C., the Athabascan people crossed the Bering Strait into Alaska. They traveled across Alaska and into what is now northern Canada. They had to learn quickly to **conquer** their new surroundings. The Athabascan people fish for salmon and hunt caribou and moose as they have for thousands of years.

They have survived by learning where to find resources that allow them to subsist. In coastal communities they hunt marine mammals, such as seals and whales, like other Inuit peoples. Inland they hunt other animals, such as musk ox.

The lives of the Athabascan people are highly adapted to their surroundings. For many thousands of years, they have endured an environment where most people would not survive.

The Inuit peoples—including the Athabasca—have hunted seals for thousands of years. This engraving shows a man in a kayak hunting a seal.

Iñupiaq

The Iñupiaq people live the farthest north of any other culture in the world. Their land is frozen for most of the year. The Iñupiaq became excellent hunter-gatherers to survive in their cold climate. They learned to hunt polar bears, caribou, seals, walruses, and even whales. They also live off the land's other natural resources, such as plants and berries.

The Iñupiaq people have continued changing their ways as time and technology advance. Today, they live very similarly to other North Americans. They have big businesses, cars, and good education systems.

Like the Chukchi, the Nenet are reindeer herders.

Nenet

The Nenet people are typically reindeer herders who live in northern Russia. The Nenet survived in their environment by traveling throughout the year. In the warmer months they would live on the tundra, and in the winter they moved south. As herders, they lived well this way.

Today, the Nenet people have to adapt their lifestyle to a world where a changing economy threatens their way of life. The mining, oil, and gas industries have harmed the local environment and made reindeer herding more difficult. Because of these changes in the environment, most Nenet people are no longer able to raise as many reindeer as they used to. Nenets will have to learn to rise to new challenges in their environment.

Saami

The Saami people can be found in Russia, Sweden, Finland, and Norway. Not much about the history of the Saami is known. They may be some of the oldest settlers of the Arctic. They were originally hunter-gatherers, similar to other peoples. Today, the Saami people and other herding communities are adjusting to new ways of life and using more and more technology. Snowmobiles and all-terrain vehicles are often used to help in herding reindeer. The herding of animals has developed into a business instead of merely a way to stay alive.

The Saami of Finland

Yup'ik

The Yup'ik people live mainly in southern Alaska and on many of the islands in the Bering Strait. They make up the majority of Alaska's Inuit peoples. Their culture is similar to that of the Chukchi.

One of the Yup'ik peoples' biggest hurdles in recent history was disease brought over by European and Russian explorers in the 1800s. However, because the Yup'ik people were so hardy, they were able to survive epidemics of smallpox, influenza, and tuberculosis.

Though the Yup'ik do get food and supplies from other people, they hunt land and marine mammals as their primary sources of food.

Years ago, the Yup'ik lived in houses built from whatever resources were available to them such as wood, whalebone, or sealskin. They speared fish from handmade boats and traded with their neighbors, the Inuit.

The Yup'ik people have changed their way of life with the coming of modern times. Modern Yup'ik people live in houses with electricity and get around in cars and all-terrain vehicles. They use electronic equipment when they fish.

Many Inuit people work with modern technology. Some use snowmobiles, like the one pictured, to travel across the snowy land.

Science and Research

Scientists have spent a lot of time studying the Arctic Circle. The Arctic aids scientific research about Earth because the cold has preserved the soil for thousands of years. Through their findings, scientists have been able to learn more about Earth's history.

In the past, scientific study was usually carried out by an **expedition.** In 1909 the first expedition reached the North Pole, the northernmost point in the Arctic Circle. Many expeditions were sent out to find a "northwest passage" that would allow a merchant or a **navigator** to travel through the icy waters of the North.

Fewer expedition ships are used these days. With enough **provisions** and sophisticated equipment for their research, scientists can spend more time in the Arctic. They can even set up permanent research facilities in strategic locations to study the Arctic environment.

The scientific study of the Arctic will lead to discoveries that may help native peoples in their changing environment. Currently, some scientists are studying the effects of oil development on caribou herds. This information will help hunters and herders to better anticipate problems in the future.

Other research is being done to investigate and **verify** heavy metal contamination in marine mammals. The more scientists find out about these potential problems, the safer native peoples will be when hunting and consuming these animals. Industries will have to comply with resulting laws and regulations that protect the Inuit way of life.

Scientists have explored the Arctic in everything from balloons to snowmobiles.

Survival in the Arctic

We have learned about how cultures have changed inside the Arctic Circle. From the Aleut to the Yup'ik people, each group has had to learn to survive in the harsh, wintry environment of the North.

It is necessary to be highly flexible if one plans to spend time there. Whether due to frigid temperatures or modern industry, native peoples are continually learning to change with their varying surroundings.

The animals and humans that have made the Arctic their home face many new challenges every day. Their territory has grown smaller with the development of land and the melting of ice due to global warming. In addition, man-made pollutants have entered the Arctic food chain.

If history is any indication of what is to come, we can rest assured that the **destiny** of people and industries is to survive—life will go on. We all share the responsibility to protect all members of society.

We must also protect our environment. This will ensure the survival of the people and animals who make their home north of the Arctic Circle.

Glossary

conquer *v.* to overcome; to get the better of.

destiny *n.* what becomes of someone or something; your fate or future.

expedition *n.* a journey for some special purpose, such as exploration, scientific study, or military purposes.

insulate *v.* to keep something from losing electricity, heat, or sound by lining it or surrounding it with a material that does not conduct the kind of energy involved.

isolation *n.* state of being separated from others; of being alone.

navigator *v.* a person in charge of finding the position and course of a ship, aircraft, or expedition.

provisions *n.* a supply of food and drink.

verify *v.* to prove to be true; to confirm.

ISBN: 0-328-13638-7

ISBN: 0-328-13638-7

4 5 6 7 8 9 10 V0G1 14 13 12 11 10 09 08 07 06

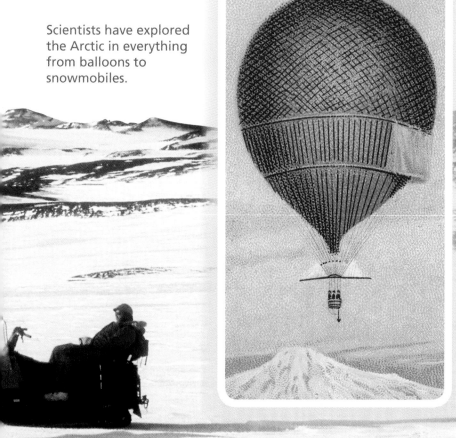